Th

CU00801538

by Wil

Preface

Last autumn, having to speak at an organ recital given by my friend Mr Clegg, I took the opportunity of giving what encouragement lay in my power, to the Corporation of my native town, in an endeavour they had made during the summer months to provide suitable music in the various parks throughout the city. To my great surprise that speech was quoted in journals, of all shades of opinion, in the country, and brought me also a vast correspondence.

A copy of the speech will be found at the end of this book.

As I have long desired that Opera should be placed within the reach of those, whose purses are not able to bear the strain of the high prices charged in England, and having some leisure before Parliament met this year, I made inquiries regarding the various systems of running Opera on the Continent of Europe. I obtained a vast mass of most interesting information. How to make the best use of that information was my difficulty. It was much too bulky to compress into the narrow limits of a magazine article, and besides, much of it had no peculiar interest for us in this country.

My chief desire was to put it before the public in a form that would arouse interest in the subject. Also, I realised that this information, however valuable, was like the desert, in its unwieldy form, and without any attempt to outline the conclusion to which it led. So after much trepidation of thought I determined to run the gauntlet and march right up to the cannon's mouth with a scheme of my own for the establishment of a system for National Opera in this country.

This little book is the result of my efforts, and though I do not pretend that it offers a complete solution of the question, still less that it gives a coup de grate to the schemes of those who have trodden the same path before me, I do hope it may help to call into existence some plan for the foundation of Opera upon a popular basis.

To my critics--and many I shall have--I venture to say that, however much they disagree, they should remember I lay no claim to completeness, and I will gladly welcome any suggestions thrown out with a real desire to perfect my very imperfect ideas.

But there are two forms of criticism I wish to meet in advance.

The first is the criticism of those, who will say it is useless hoping to get public money for a luxury, whilst the nation is engaged in a costly war. I frankly and freely admit the force of such criticism, but I would urge in reply that a proposal like mine has far to travel, before it takes its final shape, and one cannot hope to get Parliament to take the matter up until the subject has been fully ventilated in the country. And although at such a time our first thoughts should be given to those who are fighting our battles in the field, surely no harm, and possibly much good, may come from considering how we can deal with the social problems which confront us.

The second form of criticism is perhaps more easily met, namely, the criticism of those who look upon all theatres and opera houses as vicious and contra bonos mores. This battle was fought by Moliere in the seventeenth century. Prescott, in his delightful essay on Moliere, tells us what difficulties that author had to face at the beginning of his career on these very grounds. The clergy, alarmed at the then rapidly-increasing taste for dramatic exhibitions, openly denounced the theatre as an insult to the Deity, and Moliere's father anticipated in the calling his son had chosen no less his spiritual than his temporal perdition. Yet who is there to-day who will deny that Moliere helped to correct the follies of his age, by exposing them to ridicule? And if in providing National Opera for the people, we can assist in the higher education of the community, we may well ask those who object on the grounds I have named, to remember that "there is no felicity upon earth which carries not its counterpoise of misfortunes," and that the evils they fear are not inherent only to the stage, but also exist in almost every other walk of life.

The Operatic Problem

Opera has, since its origin, been considered the highest form of theatrical pastime. The very appellation "opera" indicates that in the land of its birth it was looked upon as the "work" par excellence, and to this day it is the form of Art which is invariably honoured by exalted patronage, and one that people pay the most to enjoy. It is hardly necessary to advance documentary evidence in support of this assertion; moreover, it is beyond the scope of this book to marshal all the historical facts. My chief consideration will be to deal with the prospect of National Opera in England, and to take the existing state of things as the basis for future action. But some retrospect showing that the originators of opera understood its importance, and knew admirably how to define its scope, may prove interesting.

The following extract from the preface to Vitali's Aretusa, the score of which is in the Barberini Library, performed in Rome on the 8th of February 1620, is worth quoting in corroboration of the statement:--

"This style of work (opera) is a new style, born a few years ago at Florence, of the noble intelligence of Messer Ottavio Rinuccini, who, dearly beloved by the Muses and gifted with especial talent for the expression of passions, would have it that the power of music allied to poetry, tended rather to gather fresh strength from the combination, than to suffer diminution in consequence. He spoke of it to Signor Jacopo Corsi, Menas of every merit and most enlightened amateur of music, proving that the mission of music united to poetry should be not to smother words with noises, but to help those words to a more eloquent expression of passion. Signor Corsi sent for Signor Jacopo Perri and Signor Giulio Caccini, eminent professors of singing and counterpoint, and after having discussed the subject, they came to the conclusion that they had found the means for reaching the desired goal. Nor were they mistaken. It is in this new musical style, the fable of Dafne to the poem of Signor Ottavio Rinuccini, was composed and performed in Florence at Signor Jacopo Corsi's, in the presence of the illustrious Cardinal del Monte, a Montalto, and their most serene Highnesses the Grand Duke and Grand

Duchess of Tuscany. The work pleased them so much that they were absolutely bewildered (attonitidi stupore). This style of music acquired a still greater number of fresh beauties in Euridice, a work by the same authors, and then in Ariadne, by Signor Claudio Monteverdi, to-day Maestro di Capella at Venice."

Your modern theorist could hardly express his operatic creed with greater felicity than the Florentine noble, Ottavio Rinuccini, and the whole quotation breathes in its quaint phraseology, the spirit of love for all that is new and beautiful in Art, which gave Italy her hegemony amongst other nations.

The operatic spectacle, when first imported into France, was a Court entertainment for the privileged few, but it soon tempted private enterprise, and here, again, its importance, as an attraction, was not underrated, for the first impressario, one Pierre Perrin, took good care to obtain a monopoly for the new style of performances, whilst the royal privilige (letters-patent), granted to him, sets out their advantages in unmistakable terms.[A]

Therein "Louis par la grace de Dieu," etc., concedes to his "ame et feal Pierre Perrin" the exclusive rights of operatic performances throughout France, not only that they should contribute to his own recreation, or that of the public in general, but chiefly in the hope that his subjects, "getting accustomed to the taste of music, would be led all but unconsciously to perfect themselves in this the most noble of liberal arts." (Que nos sujets s'accoustumant au goust de la musique, se porteroient insensiblement a se perfectionner en cet art, l'un des plus nobles de liberaux.) These Royal letters-patent were dated 1669, demonstrating that two hundred and thirty-two years ago France recognised the educational mission of the art of music, and its accessibility by the means of opera.

The taste for this new entertainment grew and spread throughout Europe, and it is a matter of common knowledge that everywhere the encouragement and support came from the highest quarters, always having for its object the benefit of the masses.

Thus Italy, France, Germany, Austria, Spain, Russia, Sweden, Norway, Denmark, Greece have their endowed or subsidised theatres; they can boast of an artistic musical past and operatic tradition, and make a proud show of creative and interpreting talent for over two centuries. It is equally well known that the patronage thus accorded, always took the form of a monetary subsidy granted either by a Sovereign or by a municipality--at times for a period of years, at others for a specified occasion, sometimes unconditionally, sometimes under certain restrictions, now limited to a given figure, then giving the manager carte blanche. The solicitude and favour shown by the State went at times the length of taking a direct interest in the management of an opera house, as was the case for a certain period in France.

England alone in civilised Europe remained indifferent, and took no active part either in fostering or patronising the new form of art; and whilst the spirit of emulation was animating other states and nations towards helping native production, England was satisfied to import spectacles and performers from abroad, just as she would have imported any other commodity. True enough, only the best article was brought over, and the best price paid in the highest market. If one could reckon up the money thus spent on foreign operatic performances within the last hundred years, the figures would prove instructive--instructive, that is, of England's foolhardiness in alienating so much national cash, without any benefit to the nation, and to the direct detriment of native talent. For over a century this country has been the happy dumping-ground of Italian opera and Italian singers and dancers; for there was a time when a ballet and a prima ballerina were of paramount importance in an operatic season. Within late years French, Belgian, German, American, Polish and even Dutch singers have found their El-Dorado in England. Composers of all nations have found hospitality and profit. Foreign conductors, virtuosi, teachers and chorus-singers have taken up a permanent abode here, and things have come to such a pass that one may well wonder whether there is any room at all for an Englishman, and whether the time has not arrived for a voice to be raised on behalf of native artists and native art.

It is not as though native opera had failed to show signs of life. Our failure to create a body of art comparable with that of Germany, Italy and France has sometimes been attributed to inherent lack of the dramatic instinct in music, but that view is contradicted by the historical facts. From the time of Purcell, whose operatic genius is beyond question, neither the impulse to write on the part of musicians nor the capacity to appreciate on the part of the public has been lacking. We find throughout the eighteenth and nineteenth centuries, breaking through the stifling influence of exotic art, an irrepressible tendency towards the creation of a purely native form of opera. Again and again English or British composers returned to the task with significant, if temporary, success. The list is surprisingly large and almost continuous down to the present day. It includes many forms of art, some of which have no pretension to a high standard, but the one thing common to them all is the yearning towards some sort of musical drama which they exhibit. This is seen in nothing more plainly than in the "ballad operas" of the eighteenth century, which were inaugurated by the immensely popular Beggar's Opera in 1728, only some thirty years after Purcell's flourishing period. A string of ballads took the public by storm when thrown into a dramatic setting. Arne's ambitious project of building up in the middle of the century an English operatic school to rival the Italians in their own domain indicates an instructive confidence in the forces of his day. It failed not so much from lack of support as from active opposition on the part of those undying enemies of the unaccustomed, who play the game of follow-my-leader like a flock of sheep. They did it then. They do it now.

This failure did not deter Arne's successors from freely following their own operatic bent, in the earlier and less ambitious style. The agreeable and distinctive national talent of Dibdin, Arnold, Linley, Shield, Horace, Hook, Braham and many others found expression in a host of musically set plays, which hugely delighted the public. English musicians received encouragement and responded to it. The 1809 English Opera House produced a quantity of works, and at the same time Drury Lane and Covent Garden offered a field of activity to Bishop, who was a born operatic composer of charming and original gifts. To this period belongs Balfe, who may be said to mark its culmination. The Siege of Rochelle, his first opera, was brought out at Drury Lane in 1835, and the Bohemian Girl, his most successful one, in 1843 at the same theatre. This opera has been before the public for nearly sixty years, and is still enjoying the undiminished favour of popular audiences. Wallace's Maritana, which belongs to the same period, is also very much alive to this day. Barnett's Mountain Sylph (1834) and Loder's Night Dancers (1846) met with as much success and lasted as long as four out of five contemporary Italian works, and they were only amongst the most prominent of a number of native operas, called forth in this period of sunshine and received with appreciation.

This period passed away, and has not been renewed. The promise held out by Carl Rosa, an impressario of enlightenment and enterprise, almost amounting to genius, was baulked by his premature death, and the patriotic effort embodied, in the theatre which is now the Palace Music Hall ended in worse than failure. That well-meant but disastrous venture was the heaviest blow that English opera has ever received, for it cast the shadow of hopelessness over the whole enterprise in the eyes of the public in general and the theatrical and musical world in particular. Naturally perhaps, but most unjustly.

For the general disappointment and disillusion attending the failure of Ivanhoe the critics were largely to blame in holding out expectations which could not be realised; the thing was doomed to eventual collapse from the outset. It started, it is true, with an unparalleled advertisement and amid universal good wishes; it commanded popular and fashionable patronage alike, and every adventitious attraction was provided with a lavish hand. But it lacked the essential elements of real success, and had to fight against insuperable difficulties. In the first place, the stage was far too small for grand opera, which moves in a large way, requiring large spaces. The principal characters must stand out clear, with abundant room for movement and gesture on a heroic scale. If they are huddled or crowded up against the chorus--which also requires ample space--the action is confused and leaves an impression of futility. The effect is gone. This might not altogether prevent enjoyment of a familiar work by audiences accustomed to small theatres, but it ruins the chances of a new piece conceived on a larger scale, and presented in London to playgoers accustomed to more adequate boards. The stage at the ambitious New Opera House was so small, and the foreshortening so excessive in consequence, that in the opening scene of Ivanhoe Cedric and his guests actually sat at meat in Rotherwood Hall with their knees above the table, producing a ludicrous effect. And yet the piece was projected on the most pompous scale, with tournament, siege, fire, solemn trial, battle, murder and sudden death--in short, all the details that require the most ample spaces. The reporters were told, of course, that the stage was the largest in Europe, and they may possibly have believed it. At any rate, they told the public so. They ought to have known that Ivanhoe had no chance so cramped and huddled together.

The second obstacle was the counterpart of an inadequate stage--to wit, an overloaded book. There were too many principal characters. They cluttered up the stage, got in each other's way and distracted attention from the main action. A skilful novelist can dispose of a great many characters in one story; a skilful dramatist can put fewer but still a good many into one play, because they are able to explain themselves quickly and by-play is admissible. In grand opera it is otherwise. The characters move on a higher emotional plane; they express themselves in prolonged phrases and accents enlarged beyond the manner of speech, consequently they require more time and space. It must all be simple, large and clear. There must be no distraction of interest; to have several persons of equal importance is fatal. No musician could have made a successful opera of such a book as Ivanhoe. The talent, skill and experience of Sullivan did not fail to produce some agreeable numbers, but they failed most egregiously to make grand opera. A perpetual sense of disappointment pervaded the piece; it never rose to the height demanded by the situation, save when that was comic, and occasionally the failure was absolutely painful. The music kept trying to soar, but was all the time chained by the leg. The reason is obvious. You cannot serve two masters, nor can a man who has devoted a life to light musical composition, suddenly command the powers which can only be won by toil, and tribulation, and faithful devotion to a high ideal. To crown this fabric of shortcomings, the management committed the folly of running Ivanhoe every night. No masterpiece could have stood a test of this kind. And it was thus, with this single unfortunate specimen, that English opera was to be established. Let no one be cast down by this failure. We may rather point to the attempt, to the widespread interest, and to the eager if ill-founded hopes that accompanied it, as signs of vitality. They indicate the existence of a demand, while the recurrent efforts of recent, and of still living composers--of Goring, Thomas, Corder, Stanford, Cowen, Mackenzie, M'Cunn and De Lara--prove that the dramatic instinct has not departed from British composers, and that it is not hopeless to look for a supply in answer to the demand. The seed only needs systematic encouragement, and intelligent cultivation to bear fruit. I firmly believe that the time is ripe for such encouragement to come from an official sphere; in other words, I advocate State intervention in the matter, and the establishment of a subsidised national opera house on the lines successfully adopted in other countries. And that we may profit by the experience of others, let us examine how continental nations fare under the State-aided Art.

Italy, Germany and France present the most characteristic instances, and I will take a bird's-eye view of the operatic machinery in them, beginning with Italy.

Italy

There are about five hundred theatres in Italy, and quite one half of these have seasons of opera at various times of the year. The traditional Italian operatic season begins on the 26th December of each year at San Stefano Day, and is called the Carnival Season; then follows Quaresima or Lent Season and Primavera or Spring Season--altogether some five months of opera. Besides these there exist (stagioni di fiere) short seasons of one or two weeks' duration, at the time of certain famous fairs. There are autumn seasons, and sporadic performances at fashionable summer and bathing resorts. I am quite within strict probability in asserting that in Italy two hundred odd theatres are devoted to opera the whole year round. These theatres may be briefly divided into two classes--municipal and private ones. The latter are run very much on the same lines as private theatres anywhere else, and do not come within the scope of my consideration.

The State does not interfere in any way with Italian theatres, and such help as these receive comes either from municipalities, or especially formed associations of institutions linked by common interest with the working of a theatre. But the principle of such help is always that of an act performed for the public good, or, as it is officially termed, per ragioni di pubblica utilita, and it naturally takes the form of a monetary subsidy. This varies according to the importance of the theatre, the rank of the city, the prospects of the season, and its grant is altogether opportunistic and at times arbitrary. In the majority of Italian theatres boxes are proprietary, and the palchettisti (box-holders) have a direct interest and a vote of some weight in the prospective arrangements of a season. The impressario desirous of running an operatic theatre must submit his prospectus to the box-holders at the same time he submits it to the municipality from which he wishes to obtain his contract, and of course, his subsidy. A theatrical board (Commissione Teatrale), composed of local authorities, and box-holders examines the prospectus, and if the decision is unfavourable another plan has to be submitted by the same man, or another aspirant, or perhaps the Commissione has a scheme of its own. As a rule, stipulations comprise either a novelty or a favourite opera, called in this case "obligatory" (opera d'obbligo), a ballet, or simply a specified number of performances. The length of the season varies from eight days (stagione di fiera) to two months, the repertory may consist of one opera or twenty, whilst the figure of the subsidy is anything between ?0 and ?000. The average, however, is three operas for a medium season of one month--one obligatory, one di repiego (for a change) and another, da de Stinarsi (to be selected), at the choice of the impressario or in accord with the Commissione. Five performances weekly are the orthodox number, Mondays and Fridays being recognised as days of rest.

If an agreement is arrived at, the impressario is put in possession of the theatre for the period stipulated, and sets about running his season. He is given but the bare building and seats; he has to provide scenery, costumes, orchestra and chorus in addition to his company of artists. Sometimes orchestra and chorus are local institutions, and there are small places in which the conductor is an employ?of the municipality engaged for a period of years to play the organ in church, teach music at schools, conduct open-air concerts and also the operatic season. In such a case a part of the subsidy, equivalent to all the salaries, is retained to guard against accidents, or else a sum is set apart for that purpose out of a deposit lodged by the impressario with the Commissione or the municipality.

The budget of the manager depends on the subsidy and the subscription, in which box-holders must perforce participate owing to the system of ingresso or entrance ticket--a system which consists in charging so much (a uniform price, as a rule) for entrance in addition to the price of your ticket. Ingresso simply gives you the right to standing room, or you may join some friends in a box of theirs; and this method has been devised in view of the palchettisti, whose boxes would otherwise prove a profitless asset. The palchettisti subscribe to the ingresso, and the general public to seats and ingresso combined. But the impressario does not get his subscription until he has given one-half of the stipulated performances. There is a further perquisite, called adobbo, in some southern Italian theatres--the Naples San Carlo, for instance--which brings in a goodish sum of money, and consists in charging two francs for attendance in every box. Judging from the name adobbo, it must be a relic of a time when attendance comprised some kind of "fixing" you up in your box. It is nothing of the sort to-day, and I am unable to explain why, after having paid for your box and ingresso, you are charged for the adobbo, which seems to me first cousin to the obnoxious petit banc in French theatres. Besides these two elements, subvention and subscription, the impressario has also the resource of raising the prices of seats, and entrance tickets how, and when, he pleases during the season, the fluctuation affecting, however, non-subscribers only. As a rule, the opening night of the season, and the production of a novelty are generally singled out for the adoption of this device; but, naturally enough, your manager has recourse to the measure, whenever an opera of his proves a sure draw, and results, just as much as customs, are there to justify the expedient. Should, however, the public fail to respond, the prices are lowered with the same alacrity with which they were raised. Thus you may have to pay ? for your stall, say, at La Scala, day after day, or you may see on Wednesday for 5 francs (4s.) a performance you would have had to pay 100 francs (?) for had you bought your ticket on Monday.

This principle pervades the uses and customs of the Italian theatrical world, and is applicable to the letting of scores by publishers, who, untrammelled by such institutions as the Auteurs in France, or special laws as in Spain, can charge what they please for the hire of band parts and scores. There is nothing to prevent the publisher of Lucia di Lammermoor from letting the music of the opera for 50 francs (?) to an impressario at Vigevano and charging 20,000 francs (?00) to another who produces it, say, at the Argentina of Rome, with Melba in the title-role.

The music publisher in Italy has a unique position amongst publishers, but quite apart from this, he enjoys so many prerogatives as to be almost master of the operatic situation in that country. He can put what value he pleases on the letting of the score he owns, and has the absolute right over the heads of the Theatrical Board to reject artists already engaged, including the conductor. He can take exception to costumes and scenery and withdraw his score as late as the dress rehearsal.

This is called the right of protesta. It does not follow that such right is exercised indiscriminately, spitefully or frequently, but it is sufficient that it exists, and what between the Commissione Teatrale, the palchettisti and the publisher, the impressario in Italy is not precisely on a bed of roses. Still, in spite of such impedimenta, Italian opera flourished for well-nigh two centuries, and Italian singers, repertory and language were considered all but synonymous with every operatic enterprise, during that period. This ascendency lasted as long as proper incentives for development of the art were steadily provided by responsible bodies; in other words, so long as the great theatres of Italy--La Scala at Milan, San Carlo at Naples, Communale at

Bologna, Apollo at Rome, Fenice at Venice, Carlo Felice at Genoa, Raggio [transcriber: Regio?] at Turin, Pergola at Florence, etc.--were in receipt of regular subventions. But political and economical changes in the country turned the attention of public bodies towards other channels, and the radical tendencies of most municipalities went dead against the artistic interests of the country. In spite of warnings from most authoritative quarters, the opposition, towards subsidising what was wrongly considered the plaything of the aristocracy grew apace, and the cry became common that if dukes and counts, and other nobles wanted their opera, they should pay for it. Subsidies were withdrawn here, suspended there, cut short in another place, and altogether municipal administration of theatres entered upon a period the activity of which I have already qualified, as opportunistic and arbitrary. In vain did a great statesman, Camillo Cavour, argue the necessity of maintaining at all costs, the time-honoured encouragement, and help to pioneers of the Italian opera, bringing the discussion to an absolutely practical, if not downright commercial, level. "I do not understand a note of music," said he, "and could not distinguish between a drum and a violin, but I understand very well that for the Italian nation, the art of music is not only a source of glory, but also the primary cause of an enormous commerce, which has ramifications in the whole world. I believe therefore that it is the duty of the Government to help so important an industry." The municipalities remained obdurate, and the start of their short-sighted policy coincided with the gradual decadence of Italian opera, until this form of entertainment lost prestige, and custom with the best of its former clients, England, Russia and France. We know how things on this count stand with us. In Russia, Italian opera, formerly subsidised from the Imperial purse, was left to private enterprise, and all available funds and encouragement transferred to national opera houses; whilst in France the reaction is such, that even the rare production of an Italian opera in one of the French theatres is tolerated and nothing more.

Germany

The organisation of theatres in the German Empire is quite different and widely different the results! Let us take only the Court theatres (Hoftheater), such as the opera houses of Berlin, Munich, Dresden, Wiesbaden, Stuttgart, Carlsruhe and Darmstadt in Germany, those of Vienna and Prague in Austria, and the municipal theatre of Frankfort.

These theatres are under the general direction of Court dignitaries, such as H.E. Count Hochberg in Berlin and H.S.H. Prince von Lichtenstein in Vienna, and under the effective management of Imperial "Intendants" in Vienna and Berlin, a Royal "Intendant" at Munich, Dresden, Wiesbaden, Stuttgart and Prague, Grand-Ducal at Carlsruhe and Darmstadt, and municipal at Frankfort.

The "Intendants" do not participate either in the risks or profits of the theatre, but receive a fixed yearly salary varying between 20,000 and 30,000 marks (?000 to ?500). They have absolute freedom in the reception of works, the engagements of artists, the selection of programmes and repertory, and are answerable only to the Sovereign, whose Civil List provides the subsidy, balances accounts, and contributes to the settling of retiring pensions of the personnel.

The Berlin Opera House receives a yearly subvention of 900,000 marks, or ?5,000.

The Vienna Opera House has 300,000 florins (about ?5,000) for a season of ten months. The deficit, however, if any, is made good from the Emperor's Privy Purse.

The King of Saxony puts 480,000 marks (?4,000) at the disposal of Count Intendant Seebach. It is interesting to note that in 1897 only 437,000 marks were actually spent. The orchestra of the Dresden Opera House does not figure in the budget, its members being Royal "servants" engaged for life and paid by the Crown.

At Munich it is the same, the orchestra being charged to the Civil List of the Regent of Bavaria. The cost is 250,000 marks (?2,500), and a similar sum is granted to Intendant Possart for the two theatres he manages (Hof and Residenz). The season lasts eleven months.

Wiesbaden comes next with a subvention of 400,000 marks, (?0,000) granted by the Emperor of Germany as King of Prussia. The season is of ten months' duration.

The Court Theatre at Stuttgart is open for ten months, and the Royal subvention to Baron von Putlitz, the Intendant, is 300,000 marks (?5,000).

The same sum is granted by the Grand Duke of Baden to the Carlsruhe theatre for a season of ten months.

The subvention of Darmstadt is only 250,000 marks (?2,500), the season lasting but nine months.

The States of Bohemia grant a sum of 180,000 florins (?5,000 odd) to the theatres of Prague for a season of eleven months. 100,000 florins (?000 odd) of this sum are destined for the National Tcheque Theatre.

Frankfort, as an ancient free city, does not enjoy the privileges of princely liberality, and has to put up with municipal help, which amounts to a yearly donation of 200,000 marks (?0,000) for a season of eleven months, and then the Conscript Fathers contrive to get one-half of their money back by exacting a duty of 30 pfennigs on every ticket sold. A syndicate, with a capital of ?2,500, has been formed to help the municipal institution.--Mr Claar.

The chief advantages of Court theatres consist in a guarantee against possible deficit, and freedom from taxes; and this enables the Intendants to price the seats in their theatres, in a manner which makes the best opera accessible to the most modest purse. The prices of stalls in German theatres vary between 3 and 6 marks or 3 to 4 florins. (3s. to 6s. or 7s). Other seats are priced in proportion, and a considerable reduction is made in favour of subscribers. These are simply legion, and at Wiesbaden the management have been compelled to limit their number.

The table below, shows at a glance the price of stalls in some of the chief German theatres. I give the average figure, the price varying according to the order of the row.

Vienna 4 fls. (about 7s.) Berlin 6 mks. (6s.) Munich } Wiesbaden } 5 mks. (5s.) Frankfort } Prague (Nat. Th.) 3 fls. (about 5s.) " (German Th.) 2.50 (about 4s.) Dresden } 4 mks. (4s.) Stuttgart } Darmstadt 3.50 (3s. 6d.) Carlsruhe 3 mks. (3s.)

The subscriptions are divided into four series, giving each the right to two performances weekly, but of course anyone can subscribe for more than one series. A yearly subscription comprises--at Berlin and Prague, 280 performances; at Vienna, 260; at Munich, 228; at Wiesbaden, 200; and at Frankfort, 188. To subscribers the prices of stalls are as follows:--

Vienna 3 fls. 7 kr. (6s.) Wiesbaden 5 mks. (5s.) Berlin 4.50 (4s. 6d.) Frankfort 3.51 (3s. 6d.) Munich 3.47 (3s. 6d.) Darmstadt 2 mks. (2s.) Prague 1 florin (1s. 9d.)

These figures suffice to prove the colossal benefit princely patronage and subvention bestow on the theatre-goer, in putting a favourite entertainment within the reach of the masses. Moreover, the German opera-goer is catered for both in quality and quantity.

As regards quality, he has the pick of the masterpieces of every school, nation and repertory. Gluck, Spontini, Cherubini, Auber, H 開 old, Boieldieu, Mozart, Beethoven and Weber hobnob on the yearly programmes with Wagner, Verdi, Mascagni, Puccini, Giordano and Leoncavallo, to cite a few names only. As regards quantity, the following details speak for themselves--I take the theatrical statistics for the year 1895-1896:--

The Berlin Opera House produces 60 various works--52 operas and 8 ballets.

The Vienna Opera House 74 works--53 operas and 21 ballets.

The New German Theatre at Prague--45 operas, 11 light operas and two ballets.

The Frankfort Theatre--60 operas, 11 operettes, 4 ballets and 13 great spectacular pieces.

At Carlsruhe--47 operas and 1 ballet.

At Wiesbaden--43 operas and 6 ballets.

At Darmstadt--48 operas, 2 operettes and 5 ballets.

At Hanover--37 operas.

At the National Theatre, Prague--48 operas and 6 ballets.

At Stuttgart--53 operas and 5 ballets.

At Munich--53 operas and 2 ballets.

At Dresden--56 operas, 5 ballets and 4 oratorios.

These are splendid results of enterprise properly encouraged, and I am giving only a fraction of the information in my possession, for there are no less than ninety-four theatres in Europe, where opera is performed in German, and of these seventy-nine are sufficiently well equipped to mount any great work of Wagner's, Meyerbeer's, etc.

Most of these theatres produce every year one new work at least, and thus the repertory is constantly renewed and augmented.

Every German theatre has attached to it a "choir school," where girls are admitted from their fifteenth year and boys from their seventeenth. They are taught solfeggio and the principal works of the repertory. The classes are held in the early morning, so as not to interfere with the pursuit of the other avocations of the pupils; but each receives, nevertheless, a small yearly salary of 600 marks (?0). These studies last two years, and during that time the pupils have often to take part in performances, receiving special remuneration for their services. When they are considered sufficiently well prepared, they pass an examination, and are appointed chorus-singers at a salary of 1000 to 1800 marks (?0 to ?0) a year, and are entitled besides to a special fee (Spielgeld) of 1s. 6d. to 2s. 6d. per performance for an ordinary chorus-singer, and 2s. to 5s. for a soloist. If we reckon that a chorus-singer, can take part on an average in some 250 performances in a year, at an average fee of, say, 2s. each, we find that his income is increased by a sum of ?5, a very decent competence. Nor is this all. In the smallest German towns, in the most modest theatres, there exist "pension funds" for all theatrical artists and employees. These funds are fed:--

(1.) By a yearly donation from the Sovereign's Privy Purse.

(2.) By retaining from 1 per cent. to 5 per cent. on the salaries of members.

(3.) From benefit concerts and performances.

(4.) From all kinds of donations, legacies, fines, etc.

At Stuttgart the King takes charge of all the pensions, except of those of widows and orphans, who are provided for from another fund.

At Munich the King furnishes the original capital with a sum of 200,000 marks (?0,000), and to-day the fund has over 1,000,000 marks at its disposal. Eight years' service entitles a member to a full pension.

At Prague six years' service gains a pension, but the average period throughout Germany is ten years.

There are scores of additional points of great interest, in connection with the working of German subsidised theatres. The above suffices, however, for the purpose of showing the immense advantage of a system of State-aided Art, a system that might serve as a model to a country about to embark on similar enterprises. I will add one detail more. There being no author's society in Germany, as in France, the theatrical managers treat with music publishers direct for the performing rights of scores which they own. The old repertory costs, as a rule, very little, and the rights of new works are charged generally from 5 per cent. to 7 per cent. on the gross receipts. Moreover, band parts and scores are not hired, as in Italy, but bought outright, and remain in the library of the theatre.

France

In France the State intervenes directly in theatrical matters in Paris only, subsidising the four chief theatres of the capital--to wit, the Opera, the Opera Comique, the Comie Francoise and the Odeon.

In the provinces theatres are subsidised by municipal councils, who vote each year a certain sum for the purpose. The manager is appointed for one year only, subject to his acceptance of the cahier des charges, a contract embodying a scheme of stipulations devised by the council, and imposed in return for the subsidy granted. The least infraction of the conditions laid therein brings its penalty either in the way of a fine or the forfeit of the contract. The subsidies vary according to the importance of the town, the theatres of Lyons, Bordeaux and Marseilles being the three best endowed. Less favoured are places like Rouen, Lille, Nantes, Dijon, Nancy, Angers, Reims, Toulouse, etc., and, though the Chamber of Deputies votes every year in the Budget of Fine Arts a considerable sum for the provinces, the subsidy is not allotted to theatres, but to conservatoires, symphonic concerts and orpheonic societies. Two years ago a Deputy, M. Goujon, obtained in the Chamber the vote of a special grant for such provincial theatres as had distinguished themselves by producing novelties. But the Senate threw out the proposal.

It is not, however, as if the Government of the Republic were indifferent to the fate of the provincial theatres or their progress in the field of operatic art. But worship of Paris on one side, and a dislike to decentralisation on the other, are responsible for the fact that all efforts are directed towards one channel, namely, the four before-named Parisian theatres. Of these, naturally enough only the opera house will engage my attention, or more precisely one alone, the Grand Opera House, La Theatre National de l'Opera, there being little practical difference between the working of that and of the younger house, the Theatre de l'Opera Comique.

A few words, following chronologically the various stages through which the Paris Opera House has passed since its origin, may prove of interest, and serve to indicate how untiring has been the care of successive Governments over the fortunes and the evolution of the operatic problem in France.

It will be remembered that Pierre Perrin was the possessor of the first operatic privilege granted by Louis XIV. in 1669. Hardly had he been installed when Lulli began to intrigue against his management, and having learnt that the profits of the first year amounted to over 120,000 livres, he had no rest until he obtained, through the influence of Mme. de Montespan, the dismissal of Perrin and obtained the post for himself. In fifteen years his net profits amounted to 800,000 livres!

He was succeeded by his son-in-law, Francine, who held the privilege with various fortunes until 1714, the King intervening more than once in the administration. In 1715 the Duc d'Antin was appointed Regisseur Royal de l'Academie by letters-patent of the King, who up till then considered himself supreme chief of his Academy.

In 1728 the management passed into the hands of Guyenet, the composer, who in turn made over the enterprise, for a sum of 300,000 livres, to a syndicate of three--Comte de Saint-Gilles, President Lebeuf and one Gruer. Though their privilege had been renewed for thirty years, the King, Louis XV., was obliged to cancel it owing to the scandal of a fete galante the syndicate had organised at the Academie Royale, and Prince de Carignan was appointed in 1731 inspecteur-general. A captain of the Picardy regiment, Eugene de Thuret, followed in 1733, was succeeded in 1744 by Berger, and then came Trefontain? whose management lasted sixteen months--until the 27th of August 1794. All this was a period of mismanagement and deficits, and the King, tired of constant mishaps and calls upon his exchequer, ordered the city of Paris to take over the administration of his Academy. At the end of twenty-seven years the city had had enough of it, and the King devised a fresh scheme by appointing six "Commissaires du Roi pres la Academie" (Papillon de la Ferte, Mareschel des Entelles, De la Touche, Bourboulon, and Buffault), who had under their orders a director, two inspectors, an agent and a cashier. But the combination was short-lived, lasting barely a year. In 1778 the city of Paris made one more try by granting a subvention of 80,000 livres by a Sieur de Vismos.

In 1780 the King took back from the city the operatic concession--we must bear in mind it was a monopoly all this time--appointing a "Commissaire de sa Majeste" (La Ferte) and a director (Berton).

In 1790 the opera came once more under the administration of the city, and during the troublous times of the Revolution changed its name of Academie Royale to that of Th 殁 tre de la R 闓 ublique et des Arts.

By an Imperial decree of the 29th of July 1807 the opera came under the jurisdiction of the first Chamberlain of the Emperor, whilst under the Restoration the Minister of the King's Household took the responsibilities of general supervision. One Picard was appointed director under both regimes, and was succeeded by Papillon de la Ferte and Persius. Then followed the short management of Viotti, and in 1821 F. Habeneck was called to the managerial chair.

The Comte de Blacas, Minister of the King's Household, became superintendent of Royal theatres, and after him the post was occupied by the Marquis de Lauriston, the Duc de Doudeauville and the Vicomte Sosthenes de la Rochefoucauld. Habeneck was replaced by Duplantis, who took the title of Administrator of the Opera. The administration of M. de la Rochefoucauld cost King Louis Philippe 966,000 francs in addition to the State subvention, and an extra subsidy of 300,000 francs derived from a toll levied in favour of the opera on side shows and fancy spectacles. This was in 1828, and in 1830 the King, finding the patronage of the opera too onerous for his Civil List, resolved to abandon the theatre to private enterprise. Dr Veron offered to take the direction of the opera house, at his own risk, for a period of six years with a subsidy of 800,000 francs, and, with the exception of a period of twelve years (1854-1866), the administration of the opera was included in the duties of the Master of the Emperor's Household. Both the subsidy and the principle of private enterprise have remained to this day as settled in 1830. Before then, for 151 years, French opera had enjoyed the patronage and effective help of the Sovereign, or the chief of the State, very much on the same system as obtains at the present day in Germany.[B]

Dr Veron had as successors, MM. Duponchel, Leon Pillet, Nestor Roqueplan, Perrin, Halanzier, Vaucorbeil, Ritt and Gailhard, Bertrand and Gailhard, and finally Pierre Gailhard, the present director of the Theatre National de l'Opera.

The present relations in France between the State and the director of the opera are as follows:--

The Paris Opera House, like all other theatres in France, and for the matter of that all institutions in the domain of Art in that country, is under the direct control and dependence of the Minister of Fine Arts, who has absolute power in appointing a director, in drawing up the cahier des charges, in imposing certain conditions and even in interfering with the administration of the theatre. The appointment, called also the granting of the privilige, is for a number of years, generally seven, and can be renewed or not at the wish or whim of the Minister. The cahier des charges, as already stated, is a contract embodying the conditions under which the privilige is granted. Some of these are at times very casuistic. As regards interference, one can easily understand how a chief can lord it over his subordinate if so minded. It is sufficient to point out the anomaly of the director's position who is considered at the same time a Government official and a tradesman--a dualism that compels him to conciliate the attitude of a disinterested standard-bearer of national art with the natural desire of an administrator to run his enterprise for profit. Let me cite a typical instance. Of all the works in the repertory of the opera, Gounod's Faust still holds the first place in the favour of the public, and is invariably played to full or, at least, very excellent houses, so that whenever business is getting slack Faust is trotted out as a trump card.[C] Another sure attraction is Wagner's Walke. On the other hand, a good many operas by native composers have failed to take the public fancy, and have had to be abandoned before they reached a minimum of, say, twenty performances in one year. Now, when the director sees that his novelty is played to empty houses he hastens to put on Faust or the Walke, but the moment he does it up goes a cry of complaint, and a reproof follows--"You are not subsidised to play Faust or operas by foreign composers, but to produce and uphold the works of native musicians; you are not a tradesman, but a high dignitary in the Ministry of Fine Arts," and so on.

At other times, when in a case of litigation, the director wishes to avail himself of the prerogatives of this dignity, he is simply referred to the Tribunal de Commerce, as any tradesman. Ministerial interference is exercised, however, only in cases of flagrant maladministration, and then there are, of course, directors and directors, just the same as there are Ministers and Ministers.

It is needless to go over the whole ground of the cahier des charges, the various paragraphs of which would form a good-sized pamphlet. The cardinal points of the stipulations between the contracting parties are, that the director of the Paris Opera House receives on his appointment possession of the theatre rent free, with all the stock of scenery, costumes and properties, with all the administrative and artistic personnel, the repertory, and a yearly subsidy of 800,000 francs (?2,000).

In return for this he binds himself to produce every year a number of works by native composers, and to mount these in a manner capable of upholding the highest standard of art, and worthy of the great traditions of the house. This implies, among others, that every new work must be mounted with newly-invented scenery and freshly-devised costumes, and that in general, no one set of scenery, or equipment of wardrobe, can serve for two different operas, even were there an identity of situations or historical period or any other points of similarity. Thus, if there are in the opera repertory fifty works, necessitating, say, a cathedral, a public square, a landscape or an interior, the direction must provide fifty different cathedrals, fifty different public squares, fifty varying landscapes, etc. The same principle applies to costumes, not only, of the principal artists, but of the chorus and the ballet. Only the clothes and costumes of definitely abandoned works can be used again by special permission of the Minister of Fine Arts.

As regards the new works that a director is bound to produce every year, not only is their number stipulated, but the number of acts they are to contain, and their character is specified as well. This is in order to avoid the possible occurrence of a production, say, of two works each in one act, after which exertion a director might consider himself quit of the obligation. It is plainly set out that the director must produce in the course of the year un grand ouvrage, un petit ouvrage, and a ballet of so many acts each--total, eight, nine or ten acts, according to the stipulations. Moreover, he is bound to produce the work of a prix de Rome--that is to say, of a pupil of the Conservatoire, who has received a first prize for composition, and has been sent at the expense of the Government to spend three years at the Villa Medicis of the Academie de France in Rome. Owing to circumstances, the Minister himself designates the candidates for this ex-officio distinction, guided by priority of prizes. The director had recourse to this measure through the fault of the prix de Rome themselves, who, over and over again, either had nothing ready for him or else submitted works entirely unsuitable for the house. The Minister's nomination relieves the director of responsibility in such cases.

Works of foreign composers produced at the opera, do not count in the number of acts stipulated by the cahier de charges, the respective paragraphs being drawn up in favour of native composers; nor can any excess in the number of acts produced in one year be carried over to the next year.

Amongst the prerogatives of the Paris opera director, is the absolute monopoly of his repertory in the capital--works in the public domain excepted--and the right to claim for his theatre the services of those who gain the first prizes at the final examinations of the operatic classes at the Conservatoire.

Towards the working expenses of his theatre the director has, firstly, the subvention and the subscription, and, secondly, the alea of the box-office sales. The subvention of 800,000 francs divided by the number of obligatory performances gives close upon ?70 towards each, and the subscription averages ?00 a night, or ?70 as a minimum with which the curtain is raised, and it is the manager's business to see that his expenses do not exceed the sum. The "house full" receipts being very little over ?00 at usual prices, the margin is not very suggestive of huge profits. Indeed, with the constantly rising pretensions of star artists, spoilt by the English, and American markets, and the fastidious tastes of his patrons, the Paris opera director has some difficulty in making both ends meet. Within the last fifteen years the two Exhibition seasons have saved the management from financial disaster, and this only by performing every day, Sundays sometimes included. Some fifty new works by native composers have been produced at the opera since the opening of the new house in 1876, and six by foreign composers--Aida, Otello, Lohengrin, Tannhauser, Walke, and Meistersinger. The maximum of performances falls to Romeo et Juliette, this opera heading also the figure of average receipts with 17,674 francs (about ?07). Eleven works have had the misfortune to figure only between three and nine times on the bill.

Independently of the supervision exercised by the Minister of Fine Arts, the strictest watch is kept over managerial doings by the Auteurs, a legally constituted body which represents the authors' rights, and is alone empowered to treat in their names with theatrical managers, to collect the fees, to guard the execution of contracts and even to impose fines.

Thus is national art in France not only subsidised and patronised, but safeguarded and protected.

FOOTNOTES:

[B] It may be of interest to note that during this period no less than 543 different works, mostly by native composers, had been produced. The last opera produced under the old regime on the 3rd of August 1829 was Rossini's Guillaume Tell.

[C] During 1900 Faust was played thirty-nine times to an average house of 18,397 francs (about ?30) in a repertory of twenty-five operas, and the Walke eleven times to an average of 19,417 francs (about ?77).

The English National Opera House

Three factors determine the existence of any given theatre and have to be considered with reference to my proposed National Opera House, namely, tradition, custom, and enterprise.

I have proved we possess an operatic tradition, and as regards custom no one will dispute the prevalence of a taste for opera. Indeed, from personal experience, extending over a number of years, I can vouch for a feeling akin to yearning in the great masses of the music-loving public after operatic music, even when stripped of theatrical paraphernalia, such, for example, as one gets at purely orchestral concerts. It is sufficient to follow the Queen's Hall Wagner concerts to be convinced that the flattering patronage they command is as much a tribute to the remarkably artistic performance of Mr Henry Wood, as it is due to the economy of his programmes. Again, in the provinces, I have observed, times out of number, crowded audiences listening with evident delight, not only to popular operas excellently done by the Moody-Manners' Company, but to performances of Tristan and Siegfried, which, for obvious reasons, could not give the listeners an adequate idea of the real grandeur of these works. But the love of opera is there, and so deeply rooted, that, rather than be without it, people are willing to accept what they can get.

This much, then, for tradition and custom.

As regards enterprise in the operatic field, it can be twofold--either the result of private initiative, working its own ends independently, or else it is organised, guided, and helped, officially.

It is under the former aspect that we have known it, so far, in this country, and as we are acquainted with it, especially in London, we find it wanting, from the point of view of our special purpose. Not that it should be so, for the Covent Garden management, as at present organised, could prove an ideal combination for the furtherance of national art, were its aims in accordance with universal, and, oft-expressed, desire. What better can be imagined than a theatre conducted by a gathering representative of, nobility, fashion, and wealth?

It is under such auspices that opera originated, and that native art sprang to life and prospered everywhere; and it is to these one has the right to turn, with hope and trust, in England. But when wealth and fashion stoop from the pedestal assigned to them by tradition, and barter the honoured part of Menas for that of a dealer, they lose the right to be considered as factors in an art problem, and their enterprise may be dismissed from our attention. For the aim of an opera house, worthy of a great country like England, should not be to make most money with any agglomeration of performers, and makeshift mise-en-scale, but to uphold a high standard of Art.

But the elimination of private enterprise from my scheme is but one more argument in favour of official intervention, and the experience of others will stand us in good stead.

Of the three systems of State subsidised theatres, as set out in my expos?of operatic systems in Italy, Germany, and France, the ideal one is, of course, the German, where the Sovereign's Privy Purse guarantees the working of Court theatres, and secures the future of respective personnels. But the adoption of this plan, or the wholesale appropriation of any one other, cannot be advocated, if only because the inherent trait of all our institutions is that they are not imported, but the natural outcome of historical, or social, circumstances. My purpose will be served as well, if I select the salient features of each system.

Thus, in the first instance, admitting the principle of State control in operatic matters, I will make the furtherance of national art a condition sine qua non of the very existence of a subsidised theatre, and performances in the English language obligatory.

Secondly, I will adopt the German system of prevoyance, in organising old age pensions for theatrical personnels.

Thirdly, I will borrow from Italy the idea of municipal intervention, all the more as the municipal element has become, of late, an all-important factor in the economy of our civic life, and seems all but indicated to take active part in a fresh phase of that life.

I do not see how any objection can be raised to the principle of these three points, though I am fully aware of the difficulties in the way of each; difficulties mostly born of the diffidence in comparing the status of operatic art abroad, with its actual state in this country. It must be borne in mind, however, that I am endeavouring to give help to the creation of a national art, and not promoting a plan of competition with the operatic inheritance of countries which have had such help for over two centuries.

We are making a beginning, and we must perforce begin ab ovo, doing everything that has been left undone, and undoing, at times, some things that have been, and are being, done. Let me say, at once, to avoid misapprehension, that I refer here to the majority of the Anglicised versions of foreign libretti. They are unsatisfactory, to put it very mildly, and, will have to be re-written again before, these operas can be sung with artistic decency in English. The classes of our great musical institutions will have to be reorganised entirely, from the curriculum of education to examinations. This is a crude statement of the case, the details can always be elaborated on the model of that fine nursery of artists, the Paris Conservatoire. We must not be deterred by the possible scarcity of native professors, able to impart the indispensable knowledge. Do not let us forget that the initial instructors of operatic art came from Italy to France, together with the introduction of their new art; but, far from monopolising tuition, they formed pupils of native elements, and these in turn became instructors, interpreters, or creators. The same thing will happen again, if necessary, let us by all means import ballet masters, professors of deportment, singing teachers, and whoever can teach us what we do not know, and cannot be taught by our own men. Pupils will be formed soon enough, and the foreign element gradually eliminated. Do not let us forget, either, that stalest of commonplaces that "Rome was not built in a day."

We are not trying to improvise genii, or make a complete art, by wishing for the thing, but we are laying foundations for a future architecture, every detail of which will be due to native enterprise, and the whole a national pride. To look for immediate results would be as idle as to expect Wagners, and Verdis, or Jean de Reszkes, and Terninas, turned out every year from our schools, simply because we have a subsidised opera house, and reorganised musical classes.

We are bound to arrive at results, and no one can say how great they may be, or how soon they may be arrived at. The unexpected so often happens. Not so many years ago, for example, operatic creative genius seemed extinct in the land of its birth, and the all-pervading wave of Wagnerism threatened the very existence of musical Italy, when, lo! there came the surprise of Cavalleria Rusticana, and the still greater surprise of the enthusiasm with which the work was received in Germany, and the no less astonishing rise of a new operatic school in Italy, and its triumphant progress throughout the musical world. Who can say what impulse native creative talent will receive in this country, when it is cared for as it certainly deserves?

The question arises now of the most practical manner in which this care can be exercised?

Plans have been put forward more than once,--discussed, and discarded. This means little. Any child can pick a plan to pieces, and prove its unworthiness. Goodwill means everything, and a firm conviction that in the performance of certain acts the community does its duty for reasons of public welfare. I put more trust in these than in the actual merit of my scheme, but, such as it is, I submit it for consideration, which, I hope, will be as seriously sincere, as the spirit in which it is courted.

I would suggest that the interests of the National Opera House in London, should be looked after by a Board under the supervision of the Education Department, the members of the Board being selected from among the County Councillors, the Department itself, and some musicians of acknowledged authority.

The enlisting of the interest of the Educational Department would sanction the theory of the educational mission of the venture; the County Council comes into the scheme, for financial and administrative purposes; the selection of musicians needs no explanation, but a proviso should be made that the gentlemen chosen, have no personal interest at stake.

As I said before, we have to begin at the beginning, and so the duties of the Board would be:--

1. The building of a National Opera House in London.

2. The drawing up of a schedule of stipulations on the lines of the French cahier des charges regulating the work of the theatre.

3. The appointment of a manager.

4. The supervision of the execution of the stipulations embodied in the schedule.

5. The provision of funds for the subsidy.

As to the first of these points, I do not at all agree with those who wish every new opera house constructed in servile imitation of the Bayreuth model. Such a theatre would only be available for operatic performances of a special kind, but the structure of the auditorium would result in the uniformity of prices which goes dead against the principle of a theatre meant for the masses as well as for the classes.

All that I need say here is, that our National Opera House should be built in London, and according to the newest inventions, appliances and most modern requirements.

As regards the second point, enough has been said about describing foreign systems to show how a schedule of stipulations should be drawn up, when the time comes.

Concerning the appointment of a manager, it goes without saying that the director of our National Opera House must be an Englishman born and bred, and a man of unimpeachable commercial integrity and acknowledged theatrical experience. Such a selection will make the task of the Board in supervising the work an extremely easy one.

The provision of funds is the crucial point of the scheme. Before going into details, let me appeal to the memory of the British public once more, praying that it will remember that every year some ?0,000 or ?0,000 of national cash is spent in ten or twelve weeks to subsidise French, German and Italian artistes in London. It is but reasonable to suppose that if an authoritative appeal for funds on behalf of National Opera were made, at least half of this money would be forthcoming for the purpose. And so I would advocate such an appeal as the first step towards solving the financial problem of my scheme. Secondly, there would have to be a first Parliamentary grant and an initial disbursement of the County Council funds, all towards the building of the opera house. It is impossible to name the necessary sum; but one can either proceed with what one will eventually have, or regulate expenditure according to estimates.

The house once built and the manager appointed, both Parliamentary and County Council grants will have to be renewed every year, the sum-total being apportioned to the probable expenses of every performance, the number of performances and the length of the operatic season. The best plan to follow here would be to have a season of, say nine or ten months, with four performances a week.

The manager would receive the house rent free, but should on his side show a working capital representing at least half the figure of the annual subsidy, and, further, lodge with the Board a deposit against emergencies. Considering the initial expenses of the first management, when everything, from insignificant "props" to great sets of scenery will have to be furnished in considerable quantities, there should be no charges on the manager's profits in the beginning, for a year or two. But later on, 10 per cent. off the gross receipts of every performance might be collected, one part of the proceeds going towards a sinking fund to defray the cost of the construction of the house, and the other towards the establishment of a fund for old age pensions for the personnel of the opera house.

A further source of income that would go towards indemnifying the official outlay might be found in a toll levied on the purchaser of 2d. in every 10s. on all tickets from 10s. upwards, of 1d. on tickets between 5s. and 10s., and of all tickets below 5s. I would make also compulsory a uniform charge of 6d. for every complimentary ticket given away.

It is well-nigh impossible in the present state of my scheme to go into details of figures, especially concerning the official expenditure. But, as figures have their eloquence, we may venture on a forecast of such returns as might be reasonably expected to meet the outlay. I take it for granted that our opera house will be built of sufficient dimensions to accommodate an audience of 3000, and arranged to make an average of ?00 gross receipts (subvention included) per performance possible. Taking the number of performances in an operatic season at 160 to 180, four performances a week in a season of nine or ten months, we get a total of receipts from ?12,000 to ?26,000, or, ?1,200 to ?2,600, repaid yearly for the initial expenses of the subsidising bodies, as per my suggestion of 10 per cent. taken off the gross receipts. The toll levied on tickets sold should average from ?446, 13s. 4d. to ?650 annually, with an average audience of 750 in each class of toll for each performance: altogether between ?2,646 and ?4,250 of grand total of returns. From a purely financial point of view, these might be considered poor returns for an expenditure in which items easily figure by tens of thousands. But, in the first instance, I am not advocating a speculation, and secondly, there are other returns inherent to my venture, one and all affecting the well-being of the community more surely than a lucrative investment of public funds. The existence of a National Opera House gives, first of all, permanent employment to a number of people engaged therein, and which may be put down roughly at 800 between the performing and non-performing personnel. Such is, at least, the figure at all great continental opera houses.

In Vienna, the performing personnel, including chorus, orchestra, band, ballet, supers and the principal singers, numbers close upon 400. Then follows the body of various instructors, regisseurs, stage managers, repetiteurs, accompanists, etc., then come all the stage hands, carpenters, scene-shifters, machinists, electricians, scenographers, modellers, wig-makers, costumiers, property men, dressers, etc., etc., etc., and on the other side of the footlights there are ushers, ticket collectors, and the whole of the administration. Thus one single institution provides 800 people not only with permanent employment but with old age pensions. Nor is this all. The proper working of a large opera house necessitates a great deal of extraneous aid and calls to life a whole microcosm of workers, trader manufacturers and industries of all kinds.

Let us take here the statistics for the city of Milan to better grasp my meaning. The figures are official, and are taken from a report presented to the municipality some time ago, and prove there is a business side of vital importance attached to the proper working of the local subsidised theatre, La Scala. The following are the items of what they call giro d'affari, or, in paraphrase, of "the operatic turn-over," and all are official figures.

The receipts of La Scala represent during the season the sum of 1,300,000 fr. (?2,000)

Out of which a personnel of 816, exclusive of principal artistes, receive salaries.

There are in Milan eleven operatic agencies transacting every year an average of 300,000 francs' (?2,000) worth of business, or altogether 3,300,000 fr. (?32,000)

There are nine theatrical newspapers with an average income of 15,000 francs (?00) each, or altogether 135,000 fr. (?,400)

Taking only the nineteen principal singing and ballet masters, and putting down their earnings at the modest sum of 6000 francs (?40) each, we get a total of 114,000 fr. (?,560)

The chief theatrical costumiers alone, four in number, return an average business of 80,000 francs (?200) each, or 320,000 fr. (?2,800)

Theatrical jewellers, property makers, hose manufacturers, armourers, scene-painters, may be put down for 250,000 fr. (?0,000)

The theatrical and artistic population in Milan, year in, year out, averages 3000 persons, and may be divided into three classes of 1000 persons each, according to their expenditure.

Say 1000 persons spending 4000 francs (?60) each, which makes 4,000,000 francs (?60,000); 1000 persons spending 1000 francs (?0,000); 1000 persons spending 800 francs (?2), which makes 800,000 francs (?2,000), a total of 5,800,000 fr. (?32,000)

The pianoforte dealers let about 400 instruments every year at 12 francs a month 57,800 fr. (?,312)

Taking into account only eight of the opera companies (Monte Video, New York, Caracas, Santiago, Madrid, Buenos Ayres, Rio and Lisbon) engaged in Milan, and selected exclusively from Italian artistes, we get a total of 25,525,000 fr. (?,021,000)

Adding all these together, we get a grand total of 36,801,800 fr. (?,472,072)

Very nearly a million and a half sterling turned over in operatic, business in one city. And there are scores of minor items, all sources of profit, that have to be neglected. But I must point out that no less than 1745 families derive employment and a regular income from the theatrical industry of Milan. It is quite true that the capital of Lombardy enjoys a position which is unique not only in Italy but in the whole world, as the chief operatic market, and there is nothing that indicates this artistic centre is likely to be shifted, much less to London than anywhere else. But it would be interesting to know how much English money goes towards the fine total of the Milanese operatic turn-over. There is no reason why we should not have our twenty odd trades, as in Milan, and at least 1745 households whose material existence would be definitely secured through their association with a National Opera House. If I am not writing in vain, our results should be infinitely greater, differing from continental ones as a franc or a mark differs from a pound sterling. And should the great provincial towns follow the lead of London, entrusting their municipalities with the creation and organisation of opera houses, if Manchester, Liverpool, Birmingham, Leeds, Glasgow, Sheffield, Bradford, Dublin, Hull, Southampton, Plymouth, Wolverhampton, etc., will turn a part of their wealth towards promoting a scheme of the greatest importance to the art of the nation; if all that goes to foreign pockets for foreign art is used for patriotic purposes--then England will be able to show an operatic turn-over worthy of her supremacy in other spheres. For every Italian household living on opera we will have ten, and prosperity will reign where, so far, art and an artistic education have brought only bitter disappointment. I am writing of "Music as a profession" in England. The multiplication of our music schools seems to be accepted as a great matter of congratulation, and we are perpetually hearing the big drum beaten over the increasing number of students to whom a thorough musical education has been given; but who asks what becomes of them all? Oft-met advertisements offering music lessons at 6d. an hour are perhaps an answer. It would be profitless to pursue this topic, but all will agree that it is far better to sing in an operatic chorus at 30s. or ? per week than be one of the items in a panorama of vanished illusions and struggling poverty, the true spectacle of the singing world in London.

The establishment of National Opera in England, putting artistic considerations aside, presents the following material and commercial advantages, viz., provision of permanent employment for artisans, mechanics, workmen and manual labourers; an impulse to various special industries, some developed, some improved, others created; an honourable occupation to hundreds kept out, so far, from an exclusive and over-crowded profession, and a provision for old age. In other words, the solution of the operatic problem in England might prove a step towards the solution of a part of the social problem.

That my scheme for the establishment of an English National Opera House is perfect, I do not claim for a moment. That my plans might be qualified as visionary and my hope of seeing a national art called to life through the means I advocate considered an idle dream is not unlikely.

But my conviction in the matter is sincere, and I can meet the sceptics with the words of the old heraldic motto which apologises for the fiction of a fabulous origin of a princely house: etiamsi fabula, nobilis est.

OPERA FOR THE PEOPLE

Opera for the People

The ceremony of opening a new organ, the gift of Mrs Galloway, was performed by Mr W. Johnson Galloway, M.P., in the City Road Mission Hall, Manchester, on Friday evening, September 6, in the presence of a crowded gathering. A Recital was given by Mr David Clegg.

Mr Galloway, M.P., who took the chair, in opening the proceedings, said:-- On an occasion such as this, it will not, I am sure, be deemed superfluous if I take a brief bird's-eye view of the history of music, and in a--comparatively speaking--few sentences trace its progress towards the position it now holds among the arts of modern life. Music, in one form at least, has been with us since the creation of man, for we may reasonably believe that in his most elementary stage, he discovered some vocal phrases which gave him a certain rude pleasure to repeat, or chant, in association with his fellows. Travellers, who have penetrated the confines of remote and savage countries, have told us of the curious chanting of their inhabitants when engaged in what, to them, were their religious and festal celebrations; and as we cannot conceive man in a more primitive condition, we may take it, that in prehistoric times there was a limited melodic form, which afforded that peculiar delight to the savage mind, that the glorious polyphonic combination of to-day, give to the cultured races of Eastern and Western civilisation.

Our slight knowledge of the art, in its early state we owe to such records, as have been handed down to us from that which may be termed the golden era of civilisation in Egypt. Long before the sway of the Ptolemies--ages before Cleopatra took captive her Roman Conqueror--music formed not only an indispensable part in religious and State functions, but entered largely into the social life of the people, and of this there is indisputable evidence in the hieroglyphics and carvings, to be found on the seemingly imperishable monuments, which the researches of archeologists have revealed to the knowledge of man.

Of ancient Hebrew music we do not know much, but we may assume, that during the Captivity they learned not a little from their Egyptian masters, although it does not appear--judging from the harsher and more blatant character of their instruments--that they attained the degree of refinement achieved by the Egyptians. It would seem, from the many allusions contained in the Bible, that the Jews were more particularly attracted towards the vocal, rather than the instrumental, side of the art. Many a familiar biblical phrase will probably crop up in our mind. The psalms that are sung during Divine Service teem with such references. "O sing unto the Lord a new song," "How shall we sing the Lord's song in a strange land?" are sufficient to illustrate my meaning, and among the daughters of Judea such names as Miriam, Deborah, and Judith, are especially known to us for their accomplishment in the vocal art, and as examples of the manner, in which it was cultivated by the women of Israel.

Among the ancients, however, the Greeks most assuredly had the keenest perception and appreciation of the beauties and value of music. In the Heroic age it played a significant part in their sacred games, and for a man to acknowledge an ignorance of the principles of musical art, was to confess himself, an untutored boor. In the great tragedies of Sophocles and Euripides it figured largely both vocally and instrumentally, and, even as the Welsh have their Eisteddfod, so the classic Greeks had their competitions, in which choirs from various cities strove for vocal supremacy and the honours of prize-winners.

That other great race of ancient times which fattened on the spoils of

Europe and Asia--I refer to the Romans--treated the art with less concern, and employed it in a cruder form at the celebration of their victories and Bacchanalian revels. They did little or nothing to foster or develop it, although it is said that one of their most famous--or perhaps it would be better to say infamous--rulers was so devoted to music, that he fiddled while his capital was burning. But we may reasonably have our doubts as to Nero's claim to rank as the Sarasate of his time, for although he made public appearances as a virtuoso in his chief cities, and challenged all comers to trials of skill, the importance of his recorded victories is somewhat diminished, by the fact, that his judges were sufficiently wise in their generation, to invariably award him the honour of pre-eminence. It is a prudent judge who recognises a despotic Emperor's artistic--and other--powers.

With the dawn of Christianity came a new era in the art, and in the 4th century, we find that a School of Singing was established at Rome, for the express purpose of practising and studying Church music. It was not, however, until another couple of centuries had elapsed, that the sound of music based on definite laws was heard beneath an English sky. You have to travel back in mind to that memorable procession of devoted monks, which, under the leadership of the saintly Augustine, wended its way into the little city of Canterbury, singing its Litany of the Church, and startling Pagan Britain with its joyful alleluia. Slowly, very slowly, the art progressed, but four more centuries were to pass before it was established on anything like a true scientific basis, and it is such men as Hucbald, a Flemish monk, Guido D'Arezzo and Franco of Cologne who laid the foundation of our whole system of polyphonic music.

Before, however, I touch on that broader expanse, the era of the Flemish School, which began to attain noteworthy prominence in the early years of the 15th century, it would be as well, perhaps, to dwell for a few moments on the history of the noble instrument which is the cause of our foregathering here to-day. In a very early chapter in the Book of Genesis we are told that Jubal was "the father of all such as handle the harp and the organ," and therefore he ranks in history as the first teacher of music. It is commonly asserted, that the emoluments of the modern organist do not come well within the designation of "princely," and, judging from the limited population in those Adamite days, we may well assume that Jubal's living was almost as precarious as those worthy Shetland Islanders who depended for their subsistence on washing one another's clothes. With wise forethought, however, Jubal's brother had devoted himself to engineering. "He was the instructor of every artificer in brass and iron," and therefore, we may conclude there was money in the family, and that the man of commerce was generous to the man of music, even as we of to-day are ever ready to respond to the demands for assistance, on behalf of our local choral societies, and musical organisations. But it must not be supposed, that the organ presided over by Jubal bore any resemblance whatever, to the stately instrument, which will now voice its glorious tone within these walls, for the first time in public. The primitive organ of mankind has its present-day affinity in the charming instrument, which, in the hands and mouth of a precocious juvenile, has such a powerful and stimulating effect on the cultivated ears and sensitive nerves of the modern amateur.

It is not possible for me to go into any detail, with regard to the slow and marvellous development of that triumph of human skill, which is truly known as the king of instruments. From those simple pieces of reed, cut off just below the knot, which formed the pipes of the syrinx, to the complicated, elaborate and perfect machinery which is hidden beneath the organ case there, is the same degree of difference, as there is between the rough-hewn canoe of the savage, and the wonderful perfection of the liners, which run their weekly race across the broad Atlantic. It was not until the end of the 11th century, that the first rude steps were taken towards the formation of the modern keyboard; then it was that huge keys or levers began to be used, and these keys were from 3 to 5 inches wide, 1-?inches thick, and from a foot and a half to a yard in length. Nevertheless, even the organ of the 4th century had its impressive powers, if we may place reliance on words attributed to the Emperor Julian, the Apostate, who wrote: "I see a strange sort of reeds; they must, methinks, have sprung from no earthly, but a brazen soil. Wild are they, nor does the breath of man stir them, but a blast leaping forth from a cavern of ox-hide, passes within, beneath the roots of the polished reeds; while a lordly man, the fingers of whose hands are nimble, stands and touches here and there, the concordant stops of the pipes; and the stops, as they lightly rise and fall, force out the melody."

And in its growth, as in the growth of young children, the organ has had its share of infantile vicissitudes. Even as late as the 13th century it lay under the ban of the ecclesiastics, and was deemed too profane and scandalous for Church use. Again, in 1644, Parliament issued an ordinance which commanded "that all organs and the frames and cases wherein they stand in all Churches and Chappells aforesaid shall be taken away and utterly defaced, and none other hereafter set up in their places." "At Westminster Abbey," we are told, "the Soldiers broke down the organs and pawned the pipes at several Ale Houses for pots of Ale." It is difficult to understand this opposition to the organ, more especially as David in the last of his psalms enjoined the people "to praise God with stringed instruments and organs." True, indeed, Job, in one of his most pessimistic moods, placed it on record that "the wicked rejoice at the sound of the organ," but evidently Job had no soul for music--was so unmusical, in fact, that he is worthy to be associated with a certain eminent divine of the English Church, whose musical instinct was so deficient that he only knew "God Save the Queen" was being sung by the people rising and doffing their hats.

Before touching upon that scientific development of the art, which, broadly speaking, began with the advent of the Flemish School and reached its culminating point within the rounded walls of Bayreuth, we may well give a moment's consideration to those melodies, which travelled their unwritten way through the early Middle Ages, and which we know, by the few examples that have come down to us, to have been racy of the soil that gave them birth; the folk song of the country is more characteristic of its people, of their temperament and psychology, than any other attribute of their national existence. We, in England, have little enough to point to in this way; in a sense there is nothing peculiarly individual in our music as a whole. But with the old melodies of Ireland, that ever seem to tremble between a tear and a smile, and in the quaint pathos of Scotland's airs, and the well-defined beauty of typical Welsh songs, we recognise the true speech of the heart and the outpouring of the natural man. Germany is still richer in its folk music, and the Pole and the Russian, the Hungarian and the Gaul, can each point to a mine of original melody which has provided latter-day composers with the basis of their most beautiful works. Nor must the importance of the Troubadours and Minnesingers be overlooked in reference to this interesting phase of musical art. They it was who kept alive and spread abroad the traditional songs of the people, and by their accomplishment actually worked as an educational force on the people themselves. Readers of Chaucer will bear in mind many an allusion to the minstrel's art of his period, and well through the Norman and Plantaganet epochs.

"With minstrelsy the rafters sung, Of harps, that from reflected light From the proud gallery glittered bright To crown the banquet's solemn close, Themes of British glory rose; And to the strings of various chimes Attemper'd the heroic rhymes."

To the Flemish, or Netherland School of music we owe an art system, that exercised a potent influence on every form of composition, and counterpoint was the especial study of its followers, until, as invariably happens, technical skill was regarded with a greater degree of favour than genuine inspiration. But the School unquestionably produced a vast number of very fine masses, motets, and much fine service music. Then from Belgium the musical spirit travelled to Italy, and before the 16th century had fulfilled half its appointed course, the powers of Palestrina had indelibly stamped Italian art, and his genius had elevated the ecclesiastical music of the age, to the lofty standard of its associations. Then such musicians came to mind as Monteverdi and Carissimi, the latter of whom made clear the path, for those great writers of oratorio, whose names we hold in such reverence, and whose works we love with such unwavering devotion.

German art was late in the field, and correspondingly slow in the earlier stages of its development; thus we owe it little as a pioneer in the art. But when the Teuton burst upon the world in all his greatness, he first came in the colossal personality of John Sebastian Bach, and then followed Haydn, Mozart and Beethoven, to be succeeded by others, who were well qualified to take unto themselves the mantles of their predecessors. Perhaps, however, I have done early German art some injustice, for it must not be forgotten, that to the era of the great Reformation, we owe those Lutheran chorales, such as the famous Ein' feste Burg, which were as effective in stirring and encouraging the rank and file of the reformers, as were the thrilling words of Luther, and his earnest and enthusiastic fellow-workers. And it was due to the custom of accompanying these chorales, that Germany owned, before the end of the 17th century, the finest school of organists in Europe.

English music has always leaned more towards the sacred, than the secular side of the art. The names of Marbecke, Thomas Tallis, Byrd, Farrant, Gibbons, Lawes, Blow and Purcell are known to every choir-boy and village chorister. Their anthems and chants are part and parcel of the musical programme of every parish church, and the fine example, set by these Elizabethan and Stuart writers has been well followed, by Croft, Weldon, Boyce, and nearer, and belonging to our own times, Wesley, Goss and Sullivan. And it is the sacred in music, which to-day makes the strongest appeal to the heart of the English nation. In the congregational singing in churches, in the overwhelming attention which an English audience will bestow on such an oratorio as the Messiah, we realise that a chord is struck, which vibrates through the whole of our being, which lifts us into a state of semi-exultation, and moves us like the words of some great statesman. I will not discuss the question, of whether a drama or an opera has most power over its audience, but I will fearlessly affirm, that apart from the drama there is no art that has the same soul-stirring influence, as the art of music. The simple harmonies of our Anglican hymns suffice for the untaught peasant, and the broad sweep of a Handelian chorus holds captive musical amateurism. But there is a music that reaches to higher heights, embraces within its sphere a wider domain, and goes deep down into the mysteries of nature--into the abysses of the soul; but such music is an open book only for the musical student. It lives. It exists. It swells through the length and breadth of the land; and year by year its influence increases, its power becomes more dominant, and its glowing beauties more vividly appreciated. People are beginning to comprehend the wondrous message, sent to us by such composers as Ludwig Beethoven, and Richard Wagner. They are beginning to understand the voice of that most marvellous of all instruments--more marvellous than the organ itself, for its keyboard is human brains, and its stops are human hands. I mean the modern orchestra. The world's finest music has been written for that instrument; the divinest melodies have been given it to interpret, and the most significant factor in the English art life of the present is the growing enthusiasm with which music, in its highest and most abstract form and beauty, is listened to, by those who, in political phraseology, are summed up in that terse and comprehensive expression "The Masses."

I look with much greater confidence to music, than I do to Parliament, for the means of preventing crime and intemperance--indeed, as one of the most permanent cures of all vice and discontent. Much has been done in later years by local authorities, towards enabling the public to have within easy and reasonable reach such music as can be provided by bands and local orchestra. But this is only the beginning. I trust the day may not be far distant, when local authorities will see their way to providing at cheap prices the best of operas, as is done so largely on the Continent of Europe. We rightly and wisely provide libraries, technical schools, and many other forms of instructive recreation, but why are we in England to lag behind other countries in providing that most instructive form of entertainment--namely, opera. I have never known a true lover of music who was not a good citizen. And what a preventive against idleness, the cause of so much crime. Once produce opera at a price which all can afford to pay to hear, and can anyone doubt, that many a man and woman will choose it, in preference to an evening in a public-house or a music-hall. I never remember listening to an opera, however poor or badly performed, that I have not gained some strength with which to continue the desperate struggle of the battle of life-- which is very much more than I can say, for instance, for speeches in the House of Commons. He who loves music has a servant at his command which will ever render him willing and delightful service; he who loves music brings himself into subjection, to one of the most elevating and purifying influences of civilisation, and he who loves music and will practise it, becomes a valuable and agreeable factor in the social life of the community. There are no selfish restrictions in music. The painter must keep himself to his canvas, and the actor to his stage, but singers and instrumentalists have a standing in the humble parlours of the poor, and in the luxuriously-upholstered drawing-rooms of the rich; they have a coign of vantage in the choir stalls of churches and on the platforms of concert halls. Music offers her favours alike to the modest reader of the Tonic Sol-fa Notation, and to the pianist who can master the difficulties of the Beethoven Sonatas. The chorus singer enjoys the same measure of gratification as the leading soloist, and the student with his score in his hand is just as great a king as the conductor.

In speaking briefly on such a vast and interesting subject, one must necessarily leave volumes unsaid that ought to be said. I have but casually touched on the beginnings of musical art, and the utmost I can hope for is that I have succeeded in arousing some degree of curiosity in the minds of those, who have shown but little regard for musical literature, and which will have the effect of ultimately leading them to devote more of their time and attention to good musical performances.

###

Printed in Great Britain
by Amazon.co.uk, Ltd.,
Marston Gate.